Preventing And Defending Employee Stress Claims

By Daniel Barnett

The Employment Law Library

ELS Publishing aims to publish up to two books a year in the Employment Law Library, which are sent for free to all members of the HR Inner Circle.

1. Employee Investigations
2. GDPR for HR Professionals
3. Preventing and Defending Employee Stress Claims
4. Employment Tribunal Time Limits
5. Deconstructing TUPE
6. Changing Terms & Conditions
7. Constructive Dismissal

Forthcoming:

8. Resolving Grievances

Published by Employment Law Services Limited, Unit 3, Chequers Farm, Chequers Lane, Watford, Hertfordshire WD25 0LG

ISBN 978-0-9553886-6-8

Acknowledgments

This is the third in my series of mini-guides on employment law for HR Professionals and, as always, there are a number of people I want to thank.

First and foremost, Claire Scott and Jennie Hargrove for their help with the content of this book. Claire is a first-class professional support lawyer, and Jennie is soon to qualify as a barrister with a glittering career ahead of her. Thank you both.

Christopher John Payne (google him!) is the UK's leading expert on writing and publishing small books, as well as a close friend of mine. Thank you, Chris, for all your advice.

Daniel Clarke, one of my colleagues at Outer Temple Chambers, reviewed the sections on personal injury claims - an area where his knowledge outstrips mine a hundredfold.

Thanks also to Ken Leeder and Jim Chute, for their work on the cover design and the interior layout respectively.

Finally, thank you to Miranda, Tabby, Cressie and Rufus for their love and support.

Daniel Barnett
December 2018

ABOUT THE AUTHOR

Daniel Barnett is a leading employment law barrister practising from Outer Temple Chambers. With 25 years' experience defending public and private sector employers against employment claims, he has represented a Royal Family, several international airlines, FTSE-100 companies and various NHS Trusts and local authorities. Employee clients include David & Victoria Beckham's nanny and Paul Mason (subject of the ITV documentary 'Britain's Fattest Man').

Daniel is a past chair of the Employment Lawyers' Association's publishing committee and electronic services working party. He is the author or co-author of eight books, including the Law Society Handbook on Employment Law (currently in its 7th edition). He is the creator of the Employment Law (UK) mailing list, an email alerter bulletin service sending details of breaking news in employment law three times a week to 24,000 recipients.

Legal directories describe him as 'extremely knowledgeable and [he] can absorb pages of instructions at lightning speed', 'involved in a number of highly contentious matters', 'singled out for his work for large blue-chip companies', 'combination of in-depth legal knowledge, pragmatism, quick response times and approachability', 'inexhaustible', 'tenacious', 'knowledgeable', and 'an excellent advocate'.

He is one of the leading speakers and trainers on the employment law and HR circuit. He has presented seminars for the House of Commons, the BBC, Oxford University, HSBC, Barclays Bank, Ocado, and dozens of other organisations in-house. In 2013, 2014, 2016, and 2019 he designed — and was the sole speaker at — the Employment Law MasterClass national tour.

As well as full-time practice as a barrister and speaker, Daniel is the founder of the HR Inner Circle – a membership club for smart, ambitious HR Professionals. In 2007, he co-founded CPD Webinars Ltd, then the UK's leading webinar training company for lawyers, and sold it to Thomson Reuters in 2011.

Daniel is widely sought after as a commentator in both broadcast and print media on all legal issues. Since 2010 he has presented the Legal Hour on LBC Radio.

www.danielbarnett.co.uk
Outer Temple Chambers
Strand, London

EMPLOYMENT
LAW
MATTERS

Subscribe to
Daniel Barnett's podcast

EMPLOYMENT
LAW MATTERS

via iTunes, Spotify, or your
favourite podcast player

 iTunes Spotify

Contents

Chapter 1
Introduction

According to the Health & Safety Executive, stress-related sickness absence costs the UK economy over £5 billion a year. In its report earlier this year, it described stress as a 'major cause' of sickness absence. This is against the background of the costs of general mental health problems which cost UK employers £30 billion a year, according to ACAS.

But this is not a theoretical book about stress. It's completely practical. It's written for employers. It covers the following topics:

- what stress is and what symptoms to look out for

- what you can do as an employer to minimise and prevent stress in your staff

- your duties under health and safety law, including the HSE Management Standards

- how to approach risk assessments in this area

- how you should deal with issues which may crop up with employees who are suffering from stress

- what kind of claims you may face from employees in relation to workplace stress

- personal injury claims for stress, what an employee would need to prove to be successful in a claim against you and how you might avoid them

- key messages on preventing and defending employee stress claims.

Chapter 2
What Stress is and What to Look Out For

Stress affects the individual concerned, their family and their colleagues. It also increases costs to employers who are absorbing the impact of sickness absence, replacement cover, lowered production and even increased accidents at work.

According to the World Health Organisation, 66% of the employees they surveyed said that stress made it difficult to focus, leading to mistakes, missed deadlines, lateness and trouble getting along with colleagues.

So, it's clear that as a responsible employer it is important to be aware of the impact of stress in the workplace and look at ways to reduce it.

But first, it's important to understand what stress is and what symptoms to look out for.

The HSE defines stress as "the adverse reaction people have to excessive pressures or other types of demand placed on them" at work. It isn't an illness in itself but may trigger other illnesses, including anxiety and depression and heart disease and stroke.

Stress can be as a result of many things – from work-related issues like too much work to do, or a dysfunctional relationship with a colleague, to problems in an employee's home life, such as relationship or financial problems or pressures as a result of being a carer.

It's important to remember at this stage, that pressure at work can be healthy and result in improved performance and job satisfaction. However, too much pressure can be harmful to health. The key, as always with these things, is balance.

Symptoms of stress that may crop up at work can be:

- Lower performance levels, inconsistency in performance or making mistakes;

- Loss of motivation and lack of commitment;

- Inability to make decisions and forgetting things or being evasive;

- Spending more time at work and not using holidays;

- Taking long lunches and being late, or leaving early;

- Not mixing with colleagues;

- Crying or being oversensitive;

- Being angry, irritable or moody;

- Criticising or bullying others;

- Shouting or lack of control.

This is not an exhaustive list and there may be other symptoms attributable to stress. Stress manifests differently in different people, but hopefully the above list will at least give you a starting point.

Chapter 3
How to Reduce and Prevent Stress in your Staff

So now we know what a stress reaction might look like, and how damaging it can be, what can you do as an employer to minimise or prevent it in your staff?

The first thing I would recommend is reading some of the excellent information around about stress in the workplace. ACAS have some really useful information on mental health in the workplace generally, including a great advisory booklet and a free e-learning training course.

ACAS say that managers can:

- **Spot the signs.** This may initially mean taking a note of what you see as you walk around or in team meetings and then choosing the right moment to intervene.

- **Engage with the problem.** There are some good practical steps you can take to help with coping strategies, and some legal requirements you need to bear in mind. For example, your duty to make reasonable workplace adjustments to the working environment in certain circumstances. I will look at reasonable adjustments more in TRACK 5.

- **Keep a watching brief.** In some circumstances, this can mean passively observing – but not always. HR can play an important role in promoting awareness of mental health issues and creating a culture where employees feel they can talk to you about mental health issues. Keeping communication channels open is critical, according to ACAS.

The HSE has formulated Management Standards, which set out the characteristics or culture of an organisation where the risks from work-related stress are being effectively managed and controlled. I will look at these in more detail in TRACK 4. These are really important - compliance (or perhaps more relevant, non-compliance) will be taken into account in any stress-related claim by an employee. (I will talk about claims in TRACK 7).

In addition, the HSE has a wide range of information and case studies on work-related stress for employers and employees on its website and I recommend a look.

The Trades Union Congress also has a guide to help trade union health and safety representatives work with employers to tackle workplace stress using the Management Standards.

Chapter 4
Creating A Low Stress Environment

We discussed in the previous chapter what employers can do to help or manage stress once they spot the signs. We also set out some practical steps to target the root of the problem. But what about some more general ways to look after your employees' mental health? It is important to put as many measures in place as possible. The key is to be preventative not restorative.

It won't be possible in all working environments, but where possible, it is good to encourage your employees to do some of the following:

- Take regular breaks

- Get some fresh air

- Go for a walk at lunch

- Eat away from their desk

- Talk to their co-workers

Some offices now offer short yoga and/or meditation classes during lunch to allow employees to relax and switch off for half an hour. Not all companies will have the resources to offer sessions like this, but it could prove worthwhile if it allowed your employees to feel more relaxed and like they've had a proper break.

It is also important to make your employees feel valued. Give praise where it's due, reward employees for good work and don't let their achievements go unnoticed. A positive culture is important for mental health and well-being and your employees will likely be more productive as a result. Regular one-to-one meetings can also be a great tool, they allow employers to provide feedback to the employees but also provide an opportunity for employees to give their own feedback and raise any issues that they may be having.

Top Things To Avoid

- **Unrealistic deadlines:** tight deadlines can be unavoidable at times but where possible, avoid distributing tasks with unreasonably short time frames, as it is easy for the pressure to mount if this is a regular occurrence. Employees may continually feel like they are behind or rushing, which is not good for working relationships or productivity.

- **Role ambiguity:** if an employee is not clear about their role in the company, this can make their work life more difficult. Each employee's role should be clearly defined so that they, and management, are aware what tasks/duties are their responsibility. It is easy for employees to feel burdened if they are given tasks that are outside their responsibility or expertise.

- **Inadequate training:** if an employee does not feel equipped to carry out a task, they may often be too afraid to admit that to their employer. Maintain communication and ensure that all employees have had the requisite training for their job role. Try not to make extra training feel like a punishment but a learning experience to allow them to expand the scope of their role.

- **Inadequate support:** it is important to make your employees feel valued and that they can turn to you if they are having problems. If employees do not have a good relationship with their employer it can be detrimental to their working life.

Benefits Of Tackling Stress In The Workplace

- Better working environment: when they are supported, employees will generally perform better as they have a more positive state of mind when at work.

- More effective working relationships: if things do get really bad and despite both the employer and the employee's best efforts, the workplace stress has just become too much, hopefully a good supportive working relationship will allow the situation to be resolved amicably without the need for tribunal proceedings.

- Improved levels of absence: not all employers will have the time or resources to implement all the strategies suggested, but every little helps even if it is just talking to and engaging with your employees more. At the very least your employees will feel able to discuss their issues with you more openly. You will hopefully see an increase in attendance levels and a reduction in sickness absence.

Chapter 5
Your Duties under Health & Safety Law

Employers must take care for the mental health of their employees or they may be in breach of their health and safety duties under the common law. Employers have a duty to ensure that reasonable care is taken to provide their employees with a safe place of work, safe tools and equipment and a safe system of working. Many employers will have a policy dealing with stress in the workplace. This may set out a procedure to address issues which arise. I will come on to talk more about other things you can do, in TRACK 5.

As well as case law, the Health and Safety at Work Act 1974 imposes a general duty on employers to ensure, so far as is reasonably practicable, the health, safety and welfare at work of their employees.

Under the Management of Health and Safety at Work Regulations 1999, employers are also under a duty to:

- make a suitable and sufficient assessment of the risks to health and safety which their employees are exposed to at work. This should be regularly reviewed and any significant findings recorded;

- apply 'principles of prevention' to any measures which are implemented as a result of the risk assessment. These are listed in Schedule 1 to the Regulations and include avoiding risks, combating risks at source, developing a coherent overall prevention policy covering technology, organisation of work and working conditions, social relationships and the influence of other factors relating to the working environment, and giving appropriate instructions to employees.

- Provide understandable and relevant information to employees about the identified risks to their health and safety.

So how does this fit with stress at work? Well, there are plenty of stressful situations at work which can ultimately lead to an employee going off sick with work related stress. Whether an employer is liable is a different question. I will come on to look at claims in more detail in TRACKS 7 and 8. But it's worth noting now, that just because an employee is off sick with stress, it doesn't mean that they will be successful in a stress claim against you. The key question is whether you have complied with your health and safety duties in respect of stress.

The Health and Safety Executive has developed Management Standards in six key areas of work, which you should look at in helping you manage work-related stress. These areas, if not properly managed, are associated with poor health and well-being, lower productivity and increased sickness absence. The HSE has a wealth of guidance on how to use the Management Standards.

The six areas covered are: demands, control, support, relationships, role and change. For each, the HSE sets out the standard to be achieved and what an employer should do to meet the standard. They are essentially a step-by-step risk assessment for work related stress.

Now let's delve into the detail of these HSE Management Standards.

The first one relates to 'Demands'. This is mainly about workload and exposure to physical hazards.

The Standard to be achieved by an employer is that:

- Employees indicate that they are able to cope with the demands of their job; and

- Systems are in place locally to respond to any individual concerns raised.

You achieve this Standard when:

- You provide employees with adequate and achievable demands in relation to the agreed hours of work;

- Employee's skills and abilities are matched to the job demands;

- Jobs are designed to be within the capabilities of employees; and

- Any concerns raised by employees in relation to their work environment are addressed.

An example of failing at this standard would be having employees who are not skilled or experienced enough, doing too difficult a job, working too long hours and/or not then addressing their concerns when the employee complains about it.

The second Standard is about 'Control'. This is about how much control an employee has in the way they do their work and their involvement in decision making.

The Standard to be achieved is:

- Employees feel that they have a say about the way they do their work; and

- Again, systems are in place to respond to any individual concerns.

You achieve this Standard when:

- Where possible, employees have control over their pace of work;

- Employees are encouraged to use their skills and initiative to do their work;

- They are encouraged to develop existing skills and new skills to help with new and difficult work;

- They have a say over when breaks can be taken; and

- They are consulted over their work pattern.

Performance appraisals are helpful here as is consulting with employees regularly. Giving employees an element of control in how they manage their work, when possible, can reap dividends and really help with managing stress.

The third Standard involves 'Support'. This is all about encouraging an open working environment and about the resources given to employees.

The Standard to achieve is:

- Employees feel that they receive adequate information and support from their colleagues and managers; and again, (yes you've guessed it!..)

- Systems are in place to respond to any individual concerns.

You achieve that Standard when:

- You have policies and procedures to adequately support employees. (For example, a good place to start is my HR policies pack);

- Systems are in place to enable and encourage managers to support their staff, and employees to support their colleagues;

- Employees know what support is available and how and when to access it;

- Employees know how to access the required resources to do their job; and

- Employees receive regular and constructive feedback.

Again, performance appraisals are helpful here, along with training and development at the right levels.

The fourth Standard concerns 'Relationships'. Employers need to promote positive working, to avoid conflict and deal with unacceptable behaviour like bullying and harassment.

The Standard is that:

- Employees indicate that they are not subjected to unacceptable behaviour, such as bullying, at work; and

- Systems are in place to respond to individual concerns.

The Standard is achieved when:

- You promote positive behaviour at work;

- Employees share information relevant to their work;

- You have agreed policies and procedures to prevent or resolve unacceptable behaviour. (Again, the disciplinary and grievance procedures in my policy pack are a good place to start here); and

- Systems are in place to enable and encourage employees to report and managers to deal with unacceptable behaviour.

The fifth Standard relates to making sure the employee knows their 'Role' in your organisation.
The Standard is that:

- Employees indicate that they understand their role and responsibilities; and

- That old chestnut again, that systems are in place to respond to any individual concerns.

You achieve that Standard when:

- You ensure that, as far as possible, the different requirements you place upon employees are compatible;

- You provide clear information to enable employees to understand the nature and requirement of their role and responsibilities. Job descriptions, induction and training are important here; and

- Systems are in place to enable employees to raise concerns about any uncertainties or conflicts they have in their role and responsibilities. You don't want to leave this to the grievance procedure. It's important that managers have regular meetings with their reports, to deal with issues as they come up.

The sixth and last Standard concerns 'Change' and how that is managed and communicated.

The Standard is that:

- Employees indicate that the organisation engages them frequently when undergoing an organisational change; and

- Again, systems are in place to respond to any individual concerns.

You achieve the Standard when:

- You provide employees with timely information to enable them to understand the reasons for proposed changes. You ensure adequate employee consultation on changes and provide opportunities for employees to influence proposals;

- Employees are aware of the probable impact of any changes to their jobs and are given training to support any such changes; and

- Employees know the timescales for changes and have access to relevant support during the changes.

Of course, these requirements are built into employment law in other areas such as unfair dismissal law, redundancy and TUPE, but it's helpful to think about them in the context of stress management too.

So now we know what the Management Standards are, what should we do next? In TRACK 5 I will discuss a good approach to undertaking risk assessments for work-related stress.

Chapter 6
Carrying Out Risk Assessments

Before doing a risk assessment, the HSE recommends getting the buy-in from managers, employees and trade union reps. It's also important to set up a committee, develop a project plan and communications strategy. The HSE also recommends setting aside enough resources to do the project and make sure that staff have enough time off their usual duties to get involved.

The HSE then recommends following five steps to do a risk assessment for work-related stress.

Step 1 – Identify the stress risk factors.

To do this you need to get a good understanding of the six Management Standards we talked about on Track 4. (Demands, control, support, relationships, role and change). You then need to consider how these apply to your organisation and identify specific risks.

Step 2 – Decide who might be harmed and how.

Obviously, anyone can be affected by stress. You need to gather data to assess who could be harmed by work-related stress. This might involve looking at sickness absence, productivity, performance appraisals and team meetings. You could also do anonymous staff surveys.

You should be looking at these indicators in running your business anyway, but carrying out this risk assessment involves looking at this same data through a different lens. When you analyse the data you have gathered, you can compare it against the Management Standards 'to be achieved' which I talked about in TRACK 4.

Step 3 – Evaluate the risks and develop solutions.

This is the most tricky part. Focus groups are a good way of coming up with solutions for your particular business. HSE suggests keeping groups small (6 – 10 people). It's important to listen to what people are saying and really consider any solutions proposed. HSE has useful guidance here.

Step 4 – Record findings.

This goes without saying, but drawing up an action plan and priorities is a good idea to ensure it doesn't just become a talking shop with no real progress.

Step 5 – Monitor and review the action plan and assess effectiveness.

As with all risk assessments these should be reviewed from time to time. Good times to do this are during or after periods of change such as mergers, restructures and redundancies.

Chapter 7

Dealing with Issues which crop up from Employees Suffering from Stress

In Chapter 2 I mentioned some symptoms that suggest that an employee is suffering from stress. These may first come to your attention as misconduct or poor performance.

As with all misconduct and performance procedures, you should thoroughly investigate. If there is any hint that the underlying problem is due to mental health issues and/or stress, then you should involve occupational health. If you don't do this, then any later dismissal is at risk of being unfair.

If an employee is off on long-term sickness absence, citing stress, or is behaving erratically at work, then you may need to commission a medical report. This should help you to determine what impact the condition may have on work, whether in the doctor's opinion he or she is suffering from a disability under the *Equality Act 2010*, and if so, what if any reasonable adjustments can be made. It is helpful to give clear questions and parameters to the doctor/consultant you request the report from. This will help to determine, for example, whether returning to work will affect the stress or medical condition and what needs to occur to allow a return to work. We've all seen the unhelpfully vague reports and fit notes from GPs and so it is important to try and head that off at the pass with detailed and clear questions posed in the first place.

Obviously, you need the employee's consent for a medical report. If consent is withheld then you do need to explain to the employee that without the up to date medical information, you will not have a clear picture of how to help and ultimately will have to make decisions about them, without that information. (If you are in this situation with an employee refusing consent, it is worth exhausting all options, but it can be fair to dismiss in certain situations. It's helpful to get a bit of legal advice around this).

You should consider making adjustments to the disciplinary or performance/absence management procedure even if a disability has not been identified, if stress is a factor. Don't forget to record the adjustments you make – it might be helpful if you face a claim later. I will talk about claims some more in TRACKS 7 and 8.

Here are some reasonable adjustments that could be made to the process:

- Allow more time for communication with the employee and consider different methods. You may need to remind the employee more as they

may not pick up the phone or answer letters/
emails. (Although be careful not to harass!)

- Allow a friend or family member to help the
  employee, with the employee's written consent.
  It's not ultimately a substitute for communication
  with your employee, but they may be able to
  assist with getting them to reply to letters, return
  consent forms, make doctor's appointments etc.

Sometimes an employee says that he/she doesn't
want you contacting him/her directly and that all
communication should go through someone else (often
a lawyer or spouse). If you get this sort of request it's
a good idea to seek that medical report I was talking
about before agreeing. Unless you get clear medical
evidence that contacting the employee directly will
cause further harm, be careful not to agree to no direct
communication.

Sometimes, all it takes is to agree to send letters/
emails rather than phone contact. But I have seen
employers tie themselves in knots by agreeing to no
direct communication and then trying to later progress
an absence management procedure and coming up
against a brick wall. Of course, if you get medical
evidence advising against it, you should follow that to
prevent putting your organisation at real risk of a stress
claim.

- Similarly, allowing someone who is not a
  colleague or trade union representative to attend

meetings can be helpful. Although be careful not to agree to a lawyer attending meetings!

- You may want to look at holding meetings at the employee's home or somewhere else outside the workplace; and

- Be careful and sensitive with the tone of your communications. Tribunals do not like employers who appear to disbelieve their employees when they are absent and have medical evidence to say they are ill.

When the employee is ready to come back to work, here are some reasonable adjustments to consider:

- Reduced hours and phased returns;

- Changes to start and finish times;

- Reduced workload. This is really important if the issue which caused the stress was too much work;

- Changing the type of work (although this can cause stress in itself, so always consider alongside the medical evidence and take account of what the employee says on this);

- Moving the employee to a different team. This can be important if relationships had broken down prior to absence due to behaviours as a result of the stress etc;

- Extra supervision or training;

- If the stress or mental health condition was caused by work, then it can sometimes be a reasonable adjustment to pay for treatment and counselling;

- It is not usually a reasonable adjustment to pay sick pay for longer than you would normally pay under a sickness policy. However, if the employer has caused or prolonged the absence by failing to make a reasonable adjustment that would have allowed the employee to stay at work or return to work earlier, then it might be a reasonable adjustment in those circumstances.

I GET SO FED UP WITH THE DAILY GRIND.

DANIEL
BARNETT

Chapter 8
When Does Stress Become A Disability?

It can often be difficult for employers to determine if and when stress constitutes a disability. Long term stress is not always a disability, even if there is a sick note detailing stress as the reason for the absence and making the employee unfit for work. Sick notes that refer to stress are insufficient as evidence of a long term negative effect on ability to carry out daily activities. The burden is on the employee to show the impact that stress is having on their ability to carry out day-to-day activities.

The label of stress combined with the long-term nature of an employee's absence cannot be relied upon alone to establish that an employee suffers from a disability within the legal definition. The definition of a disability is contained with Section 6 Equality Act 2010:

"a physical or mental impairment that has a 'substantial' and 'long-term' adverse effect on your ability to cary out normal daily activities".

In J v DLA Piper UK LLP UKEAT/0263/09/RN the Employment Appeal Tribunal explored this issue and drew a distinction between different types of stress. Stress can manifest itself as a result of a mental condition such as depression, and that could amount to a mental impairment as required by the Equality Act. However stress caused by an adverse life event, for example stress at work, is unlikely to be sufficient. To make the distinction a little easier, stress caused by work is also unlikely to fulfil the second requirement of longevity, as it would be unlikely to last for 12 months or more.

This distinction was also considered last year in Herry v DMC and Governing Body of Hillcrest School UKEAT/0100/16/LA. The Claimant in this case was a teacher who brought a disability discrimination claim based on his alleged stress, depression and dyslexia. He was not on any medication for stress and the occupational health report recommended he could return to work despite some "outstanding management (nonmedical) issues at the workplace which are causing stress".

The Employment Appeal Tribunal concluded that it was open to the Employment Judge to find that the Claimant was not disabled despite being certified as unfit for work due to stress. He found that the Claimant's stress was "very largely a result of his unhappiness about what he perceives to have been unfair treatment of him" and that there was "little or no evidence that his stress had any effect on his ability to carry out normal activities" (para 22).

The next chapter will explore the potential claims an employer might face, including disability discrimination.

Chapter 9
What Claims Might You Face?

There are a number of claims that an employee complaining of work-related stress can bring. In summary, these are:

- Unfair dismissal;

- Breach of contract;

- Disability discrimination;

- Personal injury; and

- Harassment, depending on the facts.

Breach of contract

Employees can also bring a breach of contract claim if they argue that the stress they are suffering from is a result of the employer's breach of their employment contract. This is often seen as a constructive dismissal claim in the employment tribunal under the Employment Rights Act 1996, but can be a stand-alone claim in the civil courts in some circumstances.

It is an implied term of every employment contract that the employer will take reasonable steps to ensure the safety of its employees at work. This includes a duty to take reasonable care not to cause psychiatric harm to an employee. It is similar to the employer's common law duty under negligence law, which I will talk about later.

A famous case involving breach of contract is Gogay v Hertfordshire County Council. Ms Gogay was suspended from her job in a children's home following allegations of child abuse. She suffered from depression and never returned to work. She was successful in claiming damages for breach of the implied term of trust and confidence, because of the Council's unreasonable decision to suspend her where there were insufficient grounds for disciplinary action. The Court of Appeal highlighted that it was possible to claim damages for psychiatric injury and not just financial loss flowing from a breach of contract.

However, in Yapp v Foreign and Commonwealth Office, the employer was not in breach of contract for the manner in which it withdrew the employee from his post, following allegations of sexual misconduct and bullying. It was not liable for damages for the depression which followed on the basis that such loss was not reasonably foreseeable. The court did say, however, that there were cases in which an employer's conduct might be so devastating that the employer should foresee that even a robust employee may develop depression as a result. So watch out!

Unfair dismissal

We are all familiar with the law on unfair dismissal, so I won't go into detail on that here. This could be someone resigning after a course of conduct and claiming constructive dismissal. Or it could be after a dismissal by the employer.

Constructive dismissal occurs where an employee feels compelled to resign following a repudiatory breach of contract by the employer. The resignation may be with or without notice but there must not be an unreasonable delay in the resignation otherwise the employee may be deemed to have affirmed the breach. A constructive dismissal will not necessarily be an unfair dismissal; the employer's conduct will be taken into account as they may be deemed to have acted fairly despite the breach of contract.

Moving away from constructive dismissal, it is possible for an employer to dismiss an employee that is suffering from stress, as long as it is a fair dismissal. A dismissal will usually be fair provided that the reason for the dismissal was one of the five potentially fair reasons set out in *s98 Employment Rights Act 1996* (conduct, capability, redundancy, breach of statutory duty or some other substantial reason) and that in all the circumstances the employer acted reasonably in treating that reason as a sufficient reason for dismissal.

The most likely context for a dismissal with someone suffering from stress is capability. This could result from either absence - it could be persistent short term, or long-term absence - or alternatively poor performance, perhaps due to an increased or difficult workload. The usual tests will apply to the procedures followed and the medical evidence taken. This often links to whether reasonable adjustments were considered. Such a claim is often brought alongside a disability discrimination claim, which I will discuss below.

Disability discrimination

Again, we are familiar with the principles here. The claim could relate to:

- Direct discrimination by treating the employee less favourably than others because of the disability.

- Treating the employee unfavourably because of something arising in consequence of disability without objective justification.

- Indirect discrimination by applying a provision, criterion or practice that disadvantages job applicants, or employees with a shared disability, without objective justification.

- Failure to make reasonable adjustments where a disabled employee is placed at a substantial disadvantage.

- Harassment related to disability.

- Victimisation because they have made/intend to make a disability discrimination claim under the Equality Act 2010, or because they have done other things in connection with the Act.

These apply to job applicants too. It is also unlawful to ask job applicants pre-employment health questions unless it relates to one of the reasons in the Equality Act.

To prove that he or she suffers from a disability, a claimant must show that he or she has a mental impairment which has a substantial and long-term effect on their day to day activities. The tribunal focuses on the effect of the alleged impairment. If it finds a long-term, substantial adverse effect, in most cases it will follow as a matter of course that the person suffers from an impairment that has produced that effect. This makes it a bit easier in practice for a claimant suffering from stress to prove he or she has a disability.

The statutory cap on unfair dismissal compensatory awards does not apply in disability discrimination claims. The claimant will normally also receive an award for injury to feelings. This can include damages for psychiatric injury as a result of the discrimination. In direct discrimination cases, the claimant doesn't need to prove that the respondent could reasonably have foreseen the extent of his/her illness. This makes it easier for a compensation award to be made than in standard personal injury cases, which I will come on to shortly.

Protection from Harassment claims can also be raised if there has been bullying and harassment (which can often cause stress).

The *Protection from Harassment Act 1997* prohibits anyone from pursuing a 'course of conduct which amounts to harassment' and which that person knows/ought to know amounts to harassment. An employer can be vicariously liable for harassment committed by its employee in the course of employment.

This kind of claim is unusual, but can actually be easier to prove than discriminatory harassment. That's because:

- There is no need to show that the course of conduct is based on a protected characteristic.

- There is no 'reasonable steps' defence available to an employer like you have under the *Equality Act*.

- Claimants have six years to bring a claim in England and Wales (which is much more than they have for discrimination and personal injury claims.) (In Scotland they only have three years to do so.)

These claims have to be brought in the civil courts, which is more expensive than tribunals (particularly now fees have been abolished in the tribunals) so this may put claimants off.

A course of conduct under the Protection from Harassment Act must be more than one incident of conduct – this differs from discrimination under the Equality Act. The conduct must be oppressive and unacceptable and have caused alarm or distress.

In *Green v DB Group Services (UK)* Ltd a negligence claim for workplace bullying was upheld by the High Court who awarded over £800,000 for bullying carried out by colleagues, which included anxiety caused by harassment. So the awards are not to be sneezed at.

This leads me on to the other main type of claim that employees can make – a personal injury claim under the law of negligence.

Personal injury claims

Court v tribunal?

The first thing to note here is that claims for psychiatric injury can't always be brought in the courts. If they relate to claims that arise out of dismissal (including constructive dismissal), then they must be brought as an unfair dismissal claim in the employment tribunal (and are therefore subject to the unfair dismissal caps on compensation).

This was made clear in the case of *Johnson v Unisys Ltd [2001] UKHL 13* – the courts must not be used to circumvent the statutory unfair dismissal procedure when it is alleged that the employer breached the implied term of trust and confidence. Such claims are deemed to fall within what is known as the Johnson exclusion area and must be brought in the employment tribunal.

However claims which arise out of events prior to and independent of the dismissal, can still be brought in the courts in exceptional circumstances. An example of a successful case brought in the courts is *Eastwood & Williams v Magnox Electric plc*; and *McCabe v Cornwall County Council and others [2004] UKHL 35*. Mr Eastwood was a security officer who was bullied and faced spurious disciplinary allegations leading to his suspension and dismissal. As a result of his manager's earlier conduct, he suffered depression. He was awarded damages in the courts as his claim stemmed from the incidents leading up to the dismissal.

In his judgment, Lord Nicholls of Birkenhead said: "If before his dismissal, whether actual or constructive, an employee has acquired a cause of action at law, for breach of contract or otherwise, that cause of action remains unimpaired by his subsequent unfair dismissal and the statutory rights flowing therefrom. By definition, in law such a cause of action exists independently of the dismissal."

If an employee brings a claim in both the employment tribunal and the courts, they cannot recover any overlapping heads of loss twice. (Which is of course positive news for employers!)

Mr Eastwood's case is nevertheless an exceptional one. Ordinarily, an employer's failure to act fairly in the steps leading to a dismissal does not of itself cause the employee financial loss. In most circumstances the loss arises following the dismissal and the claim therefore falls within the Johnson exclusion area. But as demonstrated in Mr Eastwood's case, in certain circumstances employees can claim for financial loss arising from the psychiatric harm caused by the employer's failings.

The subsequent decision in *Edwards v Chesterfield Royal Hospital NHS Foundation Trust* & *Botham v Ministry of Defence [2011] UKSC 58* went even further and extended the Johnson exclusion area to incorporate cases where the breach relied upon is a breach of the contractual disciplinary procedure. This is good news for employers as it prevents employees taking claims pertaining to the manner of dismissal through the courts unless the loss preceded and was independent of the dismissal.

So, if an employee does decide to bring a personal injury claim what must they prove? This will be addressed in detail in the next chapter.

Chapter 10
Focus on Personal Injury Stress Claims

An employer has to comply with its obligations under the health and safety legislation. And as I have already mentioned, it also has to comply with its common law duty to take reasonable care for the health and safety of employees in the workplace under the law of negligence.

The employee must show:

- That the employer has breached the duty of care owed to the employee;

- That this has caused the employee injury; and that

- An injury, of that type, was reasonably foreseeable.

The law on personal injury is a massive and complex area and you'll be delighted to hear I don't intend to go into it in a huge amount of detail. I will, however, highlight some key areas to be aware of as an employer.

The first is that the law in England and Scotland differs here, so specialist legal advice should be sought as necessary. I am going to cover this from an English law perspective. Secondly, under the law you must have Employer's Liability insurance to cover such a claim. If you are notified of a claim, you must contact your insurers immediately and follow their advice to ensure you are covered. Usually your insurers will have a panel of solicitors they use to defend claims and they will guide you here.

An employee may try and claim the employer has breached its duty to take reasonable care for his/her safety. In the context of a stress claim this usually relates to workplace bullying or too heavy a workload.

The injury suffered must be identified. Usually in stress claims the injury complained of is some form of psychiatric injury such as clinical depression or post-traumatic stress disorder. But it could also be a physical manifestation of stress, such as a heart attack. There is a big difference for personal injury purposes, between 'being stressed' and having suffered a psychiatric injury. The line can be fine and expert medical evidence is required.

Most of the time with stress claims, the case will turn on whether the psychiatric injury was reasonably foreseeable by the employer. There is no liability unless there is a real risk of harm (such as a breakdown), which the employer ought reasonably to have foreseen and which they did not avert when they should have done. This will always be fact specific and depend on what the employer knew about the employee concerned.

The employee must then show that there is a causal link between the workplace stress and the relevant injury. For example, in the case of Dickins v O2 plc, the Court of Appeal held that the employer's response to the employee's inability to cope with the demands of her new role and the lack of training given, had caused her ill health. However, in the case of MacLennan v Hartford Europe Ltd, an employee argued that she had got chronic fatigue syndrome as a result of workplace stress, but the court held that she had not proven the link between the syndrome and the workplace stress, so the claim failed.

Sutherland v Hatton guidelines

The leading case in this area is *Sutherland v Hatton*. It contains the principles to be applied when considering liability for a personal injury claim for work-related stress.

The case is long and there are many points covered. They include:

1. The legal question to be asked is whether this kind of harm to this *particular* employee (not a person of 'ordinary fortitude') as a result of their work was reasonably foreseeable.

2. Foreseeability depends on what the employer knows or ought to know about that individual employee. Unless the employer knows of some particular problem or vulnerability of that employee, then the employer is usually entitled to assume that the employee is up to the normal pressures of the job.

3. The nature and extent of the work is relevant. It will be easier to conclude that harm is foreseeable if the employer is putting unreasonable pressure upon that employee. Is the workload much more than is normal for the role? Is it particularly intellectually or emotionally demanding for this employee? Are the demands being made unreasonable, when compared to others? Are others doing that job suffering harmful levels of stress? This might be demonstrated if there is higher than average sickness absence in the team.

4. It is also relevant if there are signs from the employee (or their doctor) that unless something changes, that person is at a clear risk of a mental breakdown. However, even if there is no express warning, it might be reasonably foreseeable when looking at sickness absence, complaints made etc.

5. The reasonable steps to be taken by the employer depend on the foreseeability of the harm, the magnitude of the risk of harm occurring, the gravity of that harm, the cost and practicability of preventing it; and the justifications for running the risk.

6. Examples of reasonable steps include transferring the employee, redistributing work or providing extra help, arranging treatment or counselling or mentoring. The size and scope of the employer is relevant, as are its resources and the demands placed upon it (including the

interests of other employees.) Expert medical advice on what steps will help is required.

Hatton said that if an employer offers a confidential advice service with a referral to counselling or treatment, it is unlikely to be found in breach of duty, except where it has been placing totally unreasonable demands upon the employee, in circumstances where the risk of harm was clear. However, before you think this is the golden ticket to no liability, a subsequent case (Intel Corporation (UK) Ltd v Daw) warned employers that counselling services were not a panacea by which employers could discharge their duty of care in all cases. As always, it depends on the facts of the case. In Ms Daw's case, her employers had known she had previously had two periods of post-natal depression. Her manager found her in tears and she wrote, "I cannot sustain doing the level of work that I am currently doing… bureaucracy is stressing me out (evidenced by my violent mood swings – bad sign..have been here before – twice)..I want out". Still, management did not act and, unsurprisingly, were found liable for her injury.

In the case of *Dickins v O2* (mentioned earlier) the employer was liable for workplace stress. While her manager had referred Ms Dickens to the employer's counselling services, this was not enough when you took account that she had said to her manager that she was "at the end of her tether". So, watch out – if an employee describes severe symptoms, says it's because of stress at work and warns they can't carry on like this forever, suggesting counselling is not a good enough response.

The House of Lords in a related case, *Barber v Somerset County Council*, emphasised that the *Hatton* guidelines provided 'useful practical guidance', but do not have statutory force. It's worth looking at the facts in Barber to put the guidelines in some context though.

Mr Barber was a school teacher who took early retirement as a result of a mental breakdown. He argued that the Council was in breach of its duty of care and that his breakdown was reasonably foreseeable due to a heavy workload. He also claimed that the Council should have taken steps to try and prevent the breakdown. He did not tell his colleagues he was suffering for a few months. The first indication was when he took three weeks of work saying he was 'overstressed/depressed'.

On his return to work, nobody discussed his illness with him. He arranged meetings with his headteacher and the deputies, who were all pretty unsympathetic. They took no steps to improve or consider his situation and the following term his workload increased and sadly, he had a breakdown. The House of Lords felt that his absence for stress and depression triggered the duty to take action. At the very least, someone should have asked him about his problems and tried to reduce his workload.

According to the Judge, his condition should have been monitored, with more drastic action taken if it did not improve.

So the lesson for employers here, is to take particular care when dealing with employees absent for stress/depression etc.

Chapter 11
A Quick Word About Occupational Health

Occupational health plays a critical role in the detection and management of workplace stress. If occupational health knows about an employee's stress and the injury being caused, an employer may be held to know that information too. This depends on whether the information was provided on a confidential basis, or if the employee consented to it being provided to the employer.

Making a referral

The key thing is to make a referral as early as possible. Early referrals tend to lead to successful outcomes and the employee returning to work more quickly, with more stability. Stress can escalate and manifest in completely different ways; by tackling the problem sooner rather than later, you could find that it costs you less to resolve and hopefully the employee will return to work much quicker.

Recommendations from OH report

All sorts of reasonable adjustments could be considered; there is quite an extensive list of potential recommendations. The most likely ones to apply in situations involving stress at work are:

- Providing information in accessible formats

- Allocating some of the employee's duties to a colleague

- Offering them a suitable alternative post

- Altering hours of work

- Offering training and mentoring

- Allowing more time off for rehabilitation and treatment

- Altering performance-related pay arrangements

What's 'reasonable' will differ from organisation to organisation. Factors such as the size of the business, the cost of the adjustment and the effect of the change on the day to day running of the business would be considered.

Generally, you would expect an occupational health report to tell you:

- About any medical condition the employee has and what its effects are;

- The likely prognosis and how this will affect their ability to do their job;

- Whether or not the employee has a disability;

- Whether the employee is fit to return to work;

- If so, will they be able to do everything their role requires – with or without adjustments; and

- What should happen next.

You must take care to follow up on any occupational health recommendations, such as further assessment, or you may fail in your duty of care to the employee. The Court of Appeal made it clear in *Hartman v South Essex Mental Health Community Care NHS Trust [2005] EWCA Civ 6* that an employer who fails to act can be liable in negligence. In particular, this case highlighted that where the employer is aware that specific employees are vulnerable to stress, it is even more paramount that they don't glaze over the issues. In *Wheeldon v HSBC Bank Limited [2005] IRLR 293* the employers came under fire for ignoring the recommendations made by occupational health and closing the file without holding any discussions with the employee or implementing any changes.

Comment

Occupational health is a reactive measure, not preventative; this makes it imperative that you act promptly. The key things to take away from this are:

1. Make referrals as early as possible.

2. Ensure referrals are clear, giving all relevant information and asking the right questions.

3. Make an evidence-based response to the issue that ticks all the boxes as far as your legal responsibilities go.

Select Occupational Health Provider

Send a Referral Letter

Obtain Employee's Consent

Employee Attends OH Appointment

Employee is ready to return to work

Employee may soon be in a position to return to work

Employee is unlikely to ever fully recover and return to work

Lastly, a brief word about the working time regulations

The Working Time Regulations provide for daily and weekly rest breaks, annual leave and a 48-hour limit on the average hours worked per week. If an employer breaches these, it is going to be more difficult to defend a stress claim based on excessive working hours. However, if someone has signed an opt-out of the 48-hour limit, this may make it easier to defend.

As always it will be fact-specific though and there are previous cases in which employees were successful and unsuccessful in such claims.

Chapter 12
Myths v Facts

Stress is quite often misunderstood or underestimated, so here are a few of the most common misconceptions.

1. Stress is the same for everybody.

No. Stress manifests in different ways for different people. Responses can be emotional, physical, or a combination of both. You may not always be able to recognise the signs of stress.

2. It is obvious when someone is stressed.

Sometimes it can be obvious when an employee or colleague is feeling stressed but that will not always be the case. Many symptoms lie below the surface and people will often try hard to conceal the fact that they are suffering from stress.

3. Stress is caused by working too much

Some people can work 70 hours a week and not feel stressed; others can work 20 hours a week and suffer badly from stress. Whilst being overworked can lead to stress this does not necessarily correlate with long hours. Explore carefully with the employee what factors they (or a medical professional) think are causing their stress.

4. Stress is cured by working less

A common reaction from employers when they have an employee suffering from stress is to reduce the employee's workload, responsibilities or working hours. If this is a permanent reduction, it can have positive effects for the employee provided that the workload or hours are actually at the root of the problem.

However, if this is only a temporary solution while you wait for them to 'get better', it will not fix any underlying problems. When employees return to work or to 'normal' work conditions, nothing has changed and the stress may well return. There are lots of adjustments that can be made in the workplace, not just reduced hours. These are addressed in more detail in Chapter 7.

5. Stress is cured by working more

If an employee's stress is caused by an increased workload or by pressured deadlines, it is easy for them to rationalise that working harder for a short period of time will help them get back on top of things, with an expectation that it will go back to normal. But often this isn't the case, the longer hours and the tighter deadlines become the norm and become expected.

6. Suffering from stress makes you weak.

Sometimes stress can be seen as a sign of weakness, with people worrying that if they admit to suffering from stress they will be disregarded or considered to be a less valuable member of the team. So support your employees and make them feel appreciated, let them know that it is okay to be stressed sometimes and that you don't think any less of them for it.

7. Stress is a motivator

Stress and stimulation are not the same thing. Having targets is good, a small amount of pressure can be good; but when targets and deadlines start making your anxious and worried, it may be a sign that stimulation is turning into stress.

8. Stress is not a big deal

The severity of stress is often undervalued as the term is used so flippantly by a lot of people to describe a mildly pressured environment. If someone is suffering from severe symptoms of stress, it must be addressed.

9. If someone had a more positive attitude, they wouldn't feel stressed

This is damaging as it can lead people to believe that the fact that they are stressed is all their own fault, that their attitude is the problem, not the situation around them.

10. Minor stress symptoms are okay

It is easy to see how symptoms get ignored; headaches are a good example of a stress symptom that often seems quite minor. But there is a danger that minor symptoms will manifest into a much more serious problem.

Chapter 13
Conclusion and Top Tips

In conclusion, here are some key messages to take away on preventing and defending workplace stress claims:

1. Watch out for the signs of stress and take early action when you spot them.

2. Communicate and create an open culture where employees have ways to discuss stress and seek help.

3. Get the buy-in of management and carry out a stress risk assessment in accordance with the HSE Management Standards and Guidance.

4. Review your policies in the context of stress and consider whether a stand-alone stress policy is right for your business.

5. Make sure you put the right systems in place so employees can raise issues.

6. Consider support and reasonable adjustments when necessary.

7. Take appropriate medical advice.

8. Keep notes.

9. Notify insurers and take early legal advice if you do get a claim or think one is brewing.

Appendix I

An example of a stress policy

Introduction

We are committed to protecting the health, safety and welfare of our employees. We recognise that workplace stress is a health and safety issue and acknowledge the importance of identifying and reducing workplace stressors.

This policy will apply to everyone in the company. Managers are responsible for implementation and the company is responsible for providing the necessary resources.

Definition of stress

The Health and Safety Executive define stress as "the adverse reaction people have to excessive pressure or other types of demand placed on them". This makes an important distinction between pressure, which can be a positive state if managed correctly, and stress which can be detrimental to health.

Policy

- The company will identify all workplace stressors and conduct risk assessments to eliminate stress or control the risks from stress. These risk assessments will be regularly reviewed.

- The company will consult with Trade Union Safety Representatives on all proposed action relating to the prevention of workplace stress.

- The company will provide training for all managers and supervisory staff in good management practices.

- The company will provide confidential counselling for staff affected by stress caused by either work or external factors.

- The company will provide adequate resources to enable managers to implement the company's agreed stress management strategy.

Responsibilities

Managers

- Conduct and implement recommendations of risks assessments within their jurisdiction.

- Ensure good communication between management and staff, particularly where there are organisational and procedural changes.

- Ensure staff are fully trained to discharge their duties.

- Ensure staff are provided with meaningful developmental opportunities.

- Monitor workloads to ensure that people are not overloaded.

- Monitor working hours and overtime to ensure that staff are not overworking. Monitor holidays to ensure that staff are taking their full entitlement.

- Attend training as requested in good management practice and health and safety.

- Ensure that bullying and harassment is not tolerated within their jurisdiction.

- Be vigilant and offer additional support to a member of staff who is experiencing stress outside work e.g. bereavement or separation.

Occupational health and safety staff

- Provide specialist advice and awareness training on stress.

- Train and support managers in implementing stress risk assessments.

- Support individuals who have been off sick with stress and advise them and their management on a planned return to work.

- Refer to workplace counsellors or specialist agencies as required.

- Monitor and review the effectiveness of measures to reduce stress.

- Inform the employer and the health and safety committee of any changes and developments in the field of stress at work.

Human resources

- Give guidance to managers on the stress policy.

- Help monitor the effectiveness of measures to address stress by collating sickness absence statistics.

- Advise managers and individuals on training requirements.

- Provide continuing support to managers and individuals in a changing environment and encourage referral to occupational workplace counsellors where appropriate.

Employees

- Raise issues of concern with your Safety Representative, line manager or occupational health.

- Accept opportunities for counselling when recommended.

Safety representatives

- Safety Representatives must be meaningfully consulted on any changes to work practices or work design that could precipitate stress.

- Safety Representatives must be able to consult with members on the issue of stress including conducting any workplace surveys.

- Safety Representatives must be meaningfully involved in the risk assessment process.

- Safety Representatives should be allowed access to collective and anonymous data from HR.

- Safety Representatives should be provided with paid time away from normal duties to attend any Trade Union training relating to workplace stress.

- Safety Representatives should conduct joint inspections of the workplace at least every 3 months to ensure that environmental stressors are properly controlled.

Safety Committee

- The joint Safety Committee will perform a pivotal role in ensuring that this policy is implemented.

- The Safety Committee will oversee monitoring of the efficacy of the policy and other measures to reduce stress and promote workplace health and safety.

Signed by

Managing Director:

Date:

Employee Representative

Date:

Appendix II
Management Standards For Tackling Work Related Stress

Action plan template

Standard area	
Desired state	
Current state	
Practical solutions	
Who will take the work forward?	
When?	
How will staff receive feedback?	
Action completed?	

Appendix III
How to Tackle Work-related Stress

A guide for employers on making the Management Standards work

Introduction

Going to work is generally good for us, but only if our health, safety and welfare are protected. Preventing ill health because of work-related stress is part of creating a good working environment for your employees.

What is stress and why do we need to tackle it?

People get confused about the difference between pressure and stress. We all experience pressure regularly – it can motivate us to perform at our best. It is when we experience too much pressure and feel unable to cope that stress can result.

The Health and Safety Executive (HSE) estimates the costs to society of work-related stress to be around £4 billion each year, while 13.5 million working days were lost to stress in 2007/08. By taking action to reduce the problem, you can help create a more productive, healthy workforce and save money. Many organisations have reported improvements in productivity, retention of staff and a reduction in sickness absence after tackling work-related stress.

As an employer, you are also required by law to assess the risk of stress-related ill health arising from work activities and take action to control that risk.

What help is available?

HSE has designed the Management Standards approach to help employers manage the causes of work-related stress. It is based on the familiar 'Five steps to risk assessment' model, requiring management and staff to work together. The Standards refer to six areas of work that can lead to stress if not properly managed. They are reproduced in full at the end of this leaflet, or you can look at HSE's stress website: www.hse.gov.uk/stress.

What is the Management Standards approach?

The Management Standards approach requires managers, employees and their representatives to work together to improve certain areas of work, described

Action plan template - an example using one element of demands:

Demands	The organisation provides employees with adequate and achievable demands in relation to the agreed hours of work
Desired state	Average to good performance
Current state	Bad/very bad performance Workloads are not planned and peaks often occur during summer when people are on annual leave
Practical solutions	1. Plan the work better and if peaks do clash with fixed annual leave commitments consider talking to other departments to see if temorary resources can be provided 2. Employees to talk to line managers about upcoming leave and potential difficulties with workload during monthly meetings
Who will take the work forward?	1. Line managers to lead and suggest the idea to senior managers 2. All, with line manager to lead
When?	Issue to be raised at next senior managers meeting Immediately
How will staff receive feedback?	1. Via monthly meetings, staff bulletins 2. During monthly meetings
Action completed?	Yes. [Date] Yes – activity ongoing

in the Standards, which will have a positive effect on employee well-being.

Under each area there are 'states to be achieved', which organisations should work towards. The approach is aimed at the organisation rather than individuals, so that a larger number of employees can benefit from any actions taken.

Before you start: Prepare the organisation

Before you introduce the Management Standards approach, remember to plan ahead and prepare the organisation.

Start by thinking about securing the commitment of senior managers, line managers and employees. It is also good practice to set up a project or steering group to oversee the work.

This group will typically include senior and line managers; health and safety managers; trade union health and safety representatives or employee representatives; human resources and occupational health representatives.

What works at work?

Securing senior management commitment

The senior management team should be briefed so that they understand the rationale and business case for stress management, as well as their legal duties. Successful programmes depend on commitment from senior managers. This might be demonstrated by, for example, a director being the project sponsor, visible support from the boardroom, or senior managers attending stress management training.

> *'The Board acknowledging stress and mental health problems was an important step and created the framework for success.'*

Clive Harker, Occupational Physician, United Biscuits

Support for staff

Before the Management Standards approach is introduced, you need to make arrangements to support your staff. This may be support for line managers wanting more information about the Management Standards process, or employees wanting help to complete surveys. The steering/project group may be able to provide such support.

Step 1 — Identify the risks

Understand the Management Standards

There are six areas of work that can have a negative impact on employee health if not properly managed. These are outlined in the Management Standards, along with descriptions of good practice.

The Management Standards approach and how it applies in your workplace should be explained so that everyone understands it. Some organisations have incorporated or made reference to the Standards in their stress policy documents. This can help explain the reasons for using the approach and can define the roles and responsibilities of those involved in making the policy work.

The six Management Standards cover:

Demands – includes workload, work patterns and the work environment.

Control – how much say a person has in the way they do their work.

Support – includes the encouragement, sponsorship and resources provided by the organisation, line management and colleagues.

Role – whether people understand their role within the organisation and whether the organisation ensures that they do not have conflicting roles.

Change – how organisational change (large or small) is managed and communicated in the organisation.

Relationships – promoting positive working to avoid conflict and dealing with unacceptable behaviour.

Step 2 — Decide who might be harmed and how

Gather data

You probably already have a lot of data that can be used to identify areas of good and poor practice. Try not to rely on one set of data as this might not provide an accurate picture of your organisation. It is better to use a number of sources and look for relationships within the data to get a more accurate view of the current state of your organisation.

Annual staff surveys and/or the HSE Management Standards Indicator Tool (a questionnaire available on the HSE stress website: www.hse.gov.uk/stress) can be used to gather the views of employees. These can be used as a source of data, but should not be the only data used to assess those at risk.

The analysis of your data helps you to understand your organisation's current situation. If you have used the HSE Indicator Tool, then you can start to evaluate your data with the freely available analysis tool on the HSE stress website. This can be used as a starting point, working with employees to improve health, well-being and performance.

Typical data available includes:

- Surveys

- Sickness absence data

- Staff turnover rates

- Exit interviews

- Number of referrals to occupational health

- Information from existing staff forums

What works at work?

Communication is crucial

If staff do not understand why a survey is being done or are sceptical about its motives, they may not return questionnaires. A good return is essential to get a representative sample of the organisation. Initial communication is very important. Where there are trade union and employee representatives, they can help communicate with staff. Ways of improving response rates include delivering questionnaires with pay slips to ensure all staff get a copy and setting time aside for completion of surveys.

Existing data

Organisations with existing data tend to use this as a way to monitor progress and effectiveness. The data can then be used to strengthen arguments for activity and future initiatives.

Step 3 — Evaluate the risks

Explore problems and develop solutions

Use the results from Step 2, along with the Management Standards, to help you decide what to do in this step. Identify hot spots and priority areas. Check the results of the analysis with your employees. Then work with them to determine how to address the gap between current performance and the 'states to be achieved' within the Management Standards.

Make sure you involve employees and their representatives in discussions as they are often the ones closest to the issues and best placed to suggest improvements. A good way to consult is through focus groups – the number of groups will depend on things like the size and structure of the organisation, available resources and, most importantly, the results of your data analysis from Step 2.

The outcomes of the focus group discussions should be a set of suggested actions aimed at addressing specific issues. If you have used multiple focus groups then it is normally the role of the project team or steering group to collect and prioritise the suggested actions.

Example Standard: Demands

Demands covers issues like workload, work patterns and the work environment. The Standard here is that employees indicate that they are able to cope with the demands of their jobs, and systems are in place locally to respond to any individual concerns.

To reach this Standard, each risk area includes several points under 'What should be happening/States to be achieved'. For Demands these are:

- the organisation provides employees with adequate and achievable demands in relation to the agreed hours of work;

- people's skills and abilities are matched to the job demands;

- jobs are designed to be within the capabilities of employees; and

- employees' concerns about their work environment are addressed.

What works at work?

'Those who attended the focus groups said it was good to have a chance to talk about this aspect of their working lives and some said they found it cathartic. The focus groups also proved useful in giving practical suggestions for making simple organisational improvements.'

Gwent Health Care NHS Trust

Step — 4 Record your findings

Develop and implement action plans

It is often the case that the actions from Step 3 are aimed at different levels of the organisation such as team, department, or division and will deliver in different timescales (short, medium or long). So, when compiling your action plan, consider how you intend to evaluate each action and how you will know whether it has been successful. Ask yourself: How will we know if this is working and what measures can we use?

When complete the action plan should be communicated to employees. Some examples of popular actions are:

- Giving specific groups of employees more control over aspects of their work.

- Improving communication up and down the management chain, and between groups.

- Management development, particularly in interpersonal skills.

- Job reviews/task analysis using the Management Standards as a framework.

- Updating a specific policy or procedure shown to have failings.

What works at work?

Test decisions and policies on pilot groups

This will help you avoid the common problem that decisions made in theory can be difficult to put into practice. Also, different departments may have different problems and these need to be taken into account.

Split action plans into the six Management Standards areas

This can help you link actions back to the process, addressing 'states to be achieved'. Ensuring 'quick-wins' is also a popular option, so staff can see action is being taken.

'Action plans were developed into key themes for action around the six HSE stress risk factor categories. A leaflet outlining the

results of the stress audit and focus groups was distributed to all staff and an article written for the in-house magazine.'

Birmingham City Council

Step 5 — Monitor and review

Monitor the actions in your plan to ensure they are having the desired effect in the appropriate timescale.

At this stage reflect on what you have found out. In particular, consider what the types of activities you have put in your action plan can tell you about the underlying issues in your organisation.

Think about what you can do in the future to prevent the problems identified happening again so you are able to deal with them in a proactive rather than reactive way. Explain to managers that good stress management is not about a survey, but is an ongoing process of continuous improvement.

Remember, as with all risk assessments, record what you have done. As part of your monitoring process, you may be required to repeat the Management Standards approach again.

The essential role of the line manager

Line managers play a vital role in identifying and managing stress within the organisation. They are likely to see the problems which cause stress first hand

and will often be the first point of contact when an individual is feeling stressed. It is essential that they have the skills and behaviours to be able to manage these situations.

HSE has worked with the Chartered Institute of Personnel and Development (CIPD) and Investors in People (IiP) to commission research into the behaviours needed for an effective manager. If you have line manager responsibilities, visit HSE's stress website to try out a self-assessment survey and see if you have what it takes to manage stress at work: www.hse.gov.uk/stress/mcit.htm.

You can also visit the CIPD website for the full Line Manager Competency report: www.cipd.co.uk/guides.

The Management Standards

Demands

Includes issues like workload, work patterns, and the work environment.

The Standard is that:

- employees indicate that they are able to cope with the demands of their jobs; and

- systems are in place locally to respond to any individual concerns.

What should be happening/States to be achieved:

- the organisation provides employees with adequate and achievable demands in relation to the agreed hours of work;

- people's skills and abilities are matched to the job demands;

- jobs are designed to be within the capabilities of employees; and

- employees' concerns about their work environment are addressed.

Control

How much say the person has in the way they do their work.

The Standard is that:

- employees indicate that they are able to have a say about the way they do their work; and

- systems are in place locally to respond to any individual concerns.

What should be happening/States to be achieved:

- where possible, employees have control over their pace of work;

- employees are encouraged to use their skills and initiative to do their work;

- where possible, employees are encouraged to develop new skills to help them undertake new and challenging pieces of work;

- the organisation encourages employees to develop their skills;

- employees have a say over when breaks can be taken; and

- employees are consulted over their work patterns.

Support

Includes the encouragement, sponsorship and resources provided by the organisation, line management and colleagues.

The Standard is that:

- employees indicate that they receive adequate information and support from their colleagues and superiors; and

- systems are in place locally to respond to any individual concerns.

What should be happening/States to be achieved:

- the organisation has policies and procedures to adequately support employees;

- systems are in place to enable and encourage managers to support their staff;

- systems are in place to enable and encourage employees to support their colleagues;

- employees know what support is available and how and when to access it;

- employees know how to access the required resources to do their job; and

- employees receive regular and constructive feedback.

Relationships

Includes promoting positive working to avoid conflict and dealing with unacceptable behaviour.

The Standard is that:

- employees indicate that they are not subjected to unacceptable behaviours, eg bullying at work; and

- systems are in place locally to respond to any individual concerns.

What should be happening/States to be achieved:

- the organisation promotes positive behaviours at work to avoid conflict and ensure fairness;

- employees share information
  relevant to their work;

- the organisation has agreed policies
  and procedures to prevent or resolve
  unacceptable behaviour;

- systems are in place to enable and
  encourage managers to deal with
  unacceptable behaviour; and

- systems are in place to enable and encourage
  employees to report unacceptable behaviour.

Role

Whether people understand their role within the organisation and whether the organisation ensures that the person does not have conflicting roles.

The Standard is that:

- employees indicate that they understand
  their role and responsibilities; and

- systems are in place locally to respond
  to any individual concerns.

What should be happening/States to be achieved:

- the organisation ensures that, as far as
  possible, the different requirements it
  places upon employees are compatible;

- the organisation provides information to enable employees to understand their role and responsibilities;

- the organisation ensures that, as far as possible, the requirements it places upon employees are clear; and

- systems are in place to enable employees to raise concerns about any uncertainties or conflicts they have in their role and responsibilities.

Change

How organisational change (large or small) is managed and communicated in the organisation.

The Standard is that:

- employees indicate that the organisation engages them frequently when undergoing an organisational change; and

- systems are in place locally to respond to any individual concerns.

What should be happening/States to be achieved:

- the organisation provides employees with timely information to enable them to understand the reasons for proposed changes;

- the organisation ensures adequate employee consultation on changes and provides opportunities for employees to influence proposals;

- employees are aware of the probable impact of any changes to their jobs. If necessary, employees are given training to support any changes in their jobs;

- employees are aware of timetables for changes; and

- employees have access to relevant support during changes.

Appendix IV
Management Standards For Tackling Stress

Demands: Are you doing enough?

How much work is there?

- Ensure there are sufficient resources to do the work allocated:

  o If there are insufficient resources seek guidance from management about priorities.

  o Support your staff by helping them prioritise or renegotiate deadlines.

  o Cover workloads during staff absences.

  o Adjust work patterns to cope with peaks (needs to be fair and agreed with employees).

- If people are underloaded, think about giving them more responsibility, but make sure that they have been adequately trained.

- Strike a balance between ensuring that employees are interested and busy, but not underloaded, overloaded, or confused about the job.

- Develop personal work plans to ensure staff know what their job involves.

Are staff able to do the job?

Training and development

- Train staff so they are able to do their jobs.

- Implement personal development/training plans which require individuals to identify development/training opportunities which can then be discussed with management.

- Devise systems to keep training records up to date to ensure employees are competent and comfortable in undertaking the core functions of their job.

Communication

- Encourage staff to talk to you at an early stage if they feel as though they cannot cope.

- Develop a system to notify employees of unplanned tight deadlines and any exceptional need to work long hours.

- Talk to your team regularly about what needs to be done. This can:

- help you understand the challenges the team are currently facing and any pressures they are under;

- find ways of sharing the work sensibly and agreeing the way forward with the team;

- gain team cohesion and commitment to the work you have planned – the team is likely to be more responsive if it understands what needs to happen and by when. Allocating more work to an already stretched team without explanation is unhelpful;

- ensure shift work systems are agreed with employees and their representatives and that the shifts are fair in terms of workload;

- gain understanding and commitment to unplanned tight deadlines and any exceptional need for long hours;

- help you manage any unexpected absences or losses to the team – everyone knows the key stages of the project and what each other's role is.

- Lead by example.

How good is the work environment?

- Have a suitable and sufficient risk assessment to control physical hazards. Further information is available from HSE Infoline: 08701 545500.

- Assess the risk of physical violence and verbal abuse. Take steps to deal with this in consultation with employees and others who can help (eg the police, charities).

- Change start and finish times to help employees cope with pressures external to the organisation (eg child care, poor commuting routes).

- Ensure your risk assessments for physical hazards and risks are up to date.

- Provide training to help staff deal with and defuse difficult situations (eg difficult phone calls, aggressive members of the public).

Control: Are you doing enough?

Are you enabling staff to have their say?

- Give more control to staff by enabling them to plan their own work, make decisions about how that work should be completed and how problems should be tackled (eg through project meetings, one-to-ones, performance reviews etc).

- Allocate responsibility to teams to take projects forward:

  o Discuss and define teams at the start of the project.

  o Agree objectives and goals.

- o Agree team roles.

- o Agree timescales.

- o Agree the provision of managerial support (eg through regular progress meetings).

- Talk about the way decisions are made within the unit – is there scope for more team involvement?

Are you making full use of employees' skills and abilities?

- Enrich jobs by ensuring that staff are able to use various skills to get tasks completed, and that staff can understand how their work fits into the wider aims of the unit.

- Talk about the skills people have and if they believe they are able to use them to good effect. How else would they like to use their skills?

How much supervision is actually needed?

- Only monitor employees output if this is essential. Regular meetings with staff could be arranged to see how things are going. At these meetings managers could provide advice and support where necessary and ensure that staff are coping.

A supportive environment is crucial. Staff need to know that managers will support them, even if things go wrong or if they find that they are unable to cope with added pressures.

Support: Are you doing enough?

How supportive are you?

- Give support and encouragement to staff, even when things go wrong.

- Encourage staff to share their concerns about work-related stress at an early stage.

- Hold regular liaison/team meetings to discuss unit pressures.

- Hold regular one-to-ones to talk about any emerging issues or pressures.

- Value diversity – don't discriminate against people on grounds of race, sex or disability or other irrelevant reasons.

- Seek examples of how the team would like to, or have, received good support from managers or colleagues – can these be adopted across the unit?

- Ask how employees would like to access managerial support – 'open-door' policies, agreed times when managers are able to discuss emerging pressures etc.

How do you manage your team's time?

- Encourage a healthy work-life balance.

- Encourage staff to take their annual leave entitlement and their meal breaks.

- Include 'work-related stress/emerging pressures' as a standing item of staff meetings and/or performance reviews.

- Introduce flexibility in work schedules (where possible) to enable staff to cope with domestic commitments.

How well do you listen?

- Listen to your staff and agree a course of action for tackling any problems – it is important for staff to feel that the contribution they make at work is valued.

- Involve your staff – they need to do their bit to identify problems and work towards agreed solutions.

- Talk about ways the organisation could provide support if someone is experiencing problems outside work.

- Disseminate information on other areas of support (human resources department, occupational health, trained counsellors, charities).

How do you meet the needs of the team?

- Provide your staff with suitable and sufficient training to do their jobs.

- Give new staff a proper induction into your team and the organisation.

- Take account that people's skills and the way they approach the work will differ.

- Develop individual or unit training arrangements and refresher sessions to ensure training and competencies are up to date and appropriate for the core functions of their job.

- Offer training in basic counselling skills/access to counsellors.

- Ensure staff know how to prioritise, or how to seek help if they have conflicting priorities.

- Provide training on time management, prioritisation, assertiveness etc.

Relationships: Are you doing enough?

How well do you deal with unacceptable behaviours?

- Work in partnership with staff to ensure that bullying and harassment never emerge as an issue. One way of doing this is by having procedures in place, such as disciplinary and grievance procedures, to deal with instances of unacceptable behaviour.

- In consultation with staff and their representatives, draw up effective policies to reduce or eliminate harassment and bullying.

- Agree and implement procedures to prevent, or quickly resolve, conflict at work – communicate these to employees.

- Agree and implement a confidential reporting system to enable the reporting of unacceptable behaviour.

- Communicate the policies and make it clear that senior management fully support them.

- Communicate the consequences of breaching the policies.

Do you work for a caring organisation?

- Create a culture where members of the team trust each other and can be themselves while they are at work.

- Encourage your staff to recognise the individual contributions of other team members and the benefits of the whole team pulling together.

- Encourage good communication and provide appropriate training to aid skill development (eg listening skills, confidence building etc).

How well do you build teams?

- Select or build teams which have the right blend of expertise and experience for new projects.

- Provide training to help staff deal with and defuse difficult situations.

- Discuss how individuals work together and how they can build positive relationships.

- Identify ways to celebrate success (eg informal lunches/wash-up meetings at the end of projects).

Role: Are you doing enough?

How clear are employees about their role?

- Make sure your staff have a clearly defined role, eg through a personal work plan which enables them to understand exactly what their roles and responsibilities are.

- Encourage your staff to talk to you at an early stage if they are not clear about priorities or the nature of the task to be undertaken.

- Talk to all your staff regularly to make sure that they are clear about their current job, what it entails, what you expect of them and what they can expect from you.

Change: Are you doing enough?

Do employees understand the reasons for change?

- Ensure all staff are aware of why the change is happening – agree and implement a system for doing this.

- Explain what the organisation wants to achieve and why it is essential that the change takes place – explain the timetable for action and what the first steps are going to be. Talk about what the change will mean in terms of day-to-day activity and discuss whether there are any new training needs.

- Communicate new developments quickly to avoid the spread of rumours in the organisation. If the organisation is planning a major change your staff are likely to be discussing job security, whether they will need to relocate, and whether their terms and conditions will change.

- Face-to-face communication is generally best so that people have the opportunity to ask questions and say what they feel, but any means (eg paper, electronic) would be helpful.

- Have an open-door policy where staff can talk to you about their concerns or any suggestions they have for improving the way change is managed.

Have staff been involved in the changes?
- Provide a confidential system to enable staff to comment and ask questions before, during and after the change.

- Involve staff in discussions about how jobs might be developed and changed and in generating ways of solving problems.

- Supporting your staff is essential during a change.

- Involve staff in discussions about how jobs might be developed and changed.

- Have an 'open-door' policy to help staff who want to talk to their managers about their concerns.

How can you help staff adversely affected by change?

- Ensure that staff are aware of the impact of the change on their jobs.

- Help staff who are to be made redundant by the change by giving them the skills they need to find a new job, for example by helping them to write a CV and prepare for interviews.

- After the change think about revising work objectives to avoid role conflict and role ambiguity.

- Revise your risk assessment/action plans to see if any changes, for example a decrease in staff numbers, have resulted in increased hazards to staff. Remember that social changes (eg if staff are now working with a completely different group of people) may have more of an impact on the individual than technological or geographical changes.

- Hold team meetings to enable team members to clarify their role and discuss any possible role conflict.

- Display team/department targets and objectives to help clarify the role of the unit and the individual.

How well do you manage new recruits?

- Make sure that new members of staff receive a comprehensive induction into your organisation. If this is not arranged centrally, you should do it locally.

- If your organisation has gone through change, check with members of your team to make sure they understand their new roles and are comfortable with them.

- Develop suitable induction arrangements for new staff – make sure all members of the team understand the role and responsibilities of the new recruit.

Do employees understand what you expect from them?

- Agree specific standards of performance for jobs and individual tasks and review periodically.

- Introduce personal work plans which are aligned to the outputs of the unit.

- Introduce or revise job descriptions to help ensure that the core functions and priorities of the post are clear.

- Hold regular one-to-one meetings to ensure that individuals are clear about their role and know what is planned for the coming months.

Also by
Daniel Barnett

Available on Amazon

JOIN DANIEL EVERY SATURDAY EVENING AT
9PM WHEN HE PRESENTS THE ALL-NEW

LBC LEGAL HOUR

— OR CATCH UP VIA THE GLOBAL PLAYER,
AT bit.ly/lbclegalhour

SATURDAYS, 9PM

I have updated my 20 Employment Law Policies for small businesses.

If you are an HR professional, they are perfect for incorporating into a staff handbook. If you are a solicitor, they come with a licence for you to resell them or give them away for free to clients.

WWW.POLICIES2020.COM

HR INNER CIRCLE

"The HR Inner Circle has improved my life amazingly, mainly because it means I have to spend less time researching and more time and more time actually doing the work I'm paid for."

Sue Whittle, Employment & Safety Advice LTD

Join to gain access to the monthly HR Inner Circular magazine

jam-packed with amazing information for ambitious HR professionals

WWW.HRINNERCIRCLE.CO.UK

What do you get?

1 Monthly live online 'Ask Me Anything' sessions: each month, we host an online video webinar, when you can share your HR problems and ask Daniel anything about employment law. You'll also receive a recording and a transcript each month, so you have a permanent record of the session even if you cannot be there.

Please ask your questions now:
1. click 'Raise Hand'; or,
2. type it into the Questions box

"Daniel Barnett is an inspirational, walking and talking 'how to understand mind-boggling employment law handbook!"

Ellie King, HR Manager, RWE Technology

2 A specially recorded audio seminar every month, with HR shortcuts and workarounds you can't get anywhere else.

WWW.HRINNERCIRCLE.CO.UK

3   The monthly Inner Circular magazine, jam-packed with valuable information for ambitious HR professionals.

4   Access to Daniel's exclusive, private, invitation-only online Inner Circle group, where you get to discuss HR problems with other smart, ambitious professionals and download precedents and policies they have shared.

"It's the support and help that you get, the reassurance that you're talking to people who know what they're talking about rather than people just randomly giving information."

Nicky Jolley, HR2DAY LTD

5   Access to the exclusive HR Inner Circle website which includes a back-catalogue of all the HRIC resources since the launch in 2015.

WWW.HRINNERCIRCLE.CO.UK

"This is one of the best investments in yourself and your career you will ever decide to take."

If you are looking for a forum to discuss confidential issues that need prompt employment law advice, then the HR Inner Circle is definitely for you. In addition it offers other tools to help and support. The Facebook group is full of information and solutions to scenarios — invaluable for HR professionals.

- **Sheena Doyle**, Managing Director, The Really Useful HR Company Ltd

---

It's a forum where you're not afraid to ask stupid questions, even though I'm not usually afraid of doing that. The sheer variety of experience and skillsets ensures there is always an informed discussion. JOIN NOW!!

- **Jon Dews**, HR & Business Partner, Majestic 12 Ltd

If you are looking for a steady stream of thorough, pragmatic, and easily-digestible employment law advice, the HR Inner Circle is a great place to be.

- **Susi O'Brien**, Senior Manager HR, The Action Group

The regular updates are invaluable to not only me, but also my team. We find that they are presented in an easy to digest format and aren't too 'legalistic'.

- **Donna Negus**, Sekoya Specialist Employment Services

WWW.HRINNERCIRCLE.CO.UK

There aren't many other employment law advice services where you get direct access to an employment law barrister at a realistic price. Join the HR Inner Circle now – you won't regret it.

- **Kirsten Cluer**, Owner of Cluer HR, HR Consultancy

I like being able to use the HR Inner Circle Facebook group to ask other members for a second opinion, or for ideas when I get stuck with solving a tricky situation. There's usually someone who has come across the situation before.

- **Helen Astill**, Managing Director, Cherington HR Ltd

When I transitioned from big employers to an SME, I didn't realise how much I would miss having peers to kick ideas around. If you haven't got an internal network, you've got to build an external one. I got so much out of the discussion at an Inner Circle meetup recently and I look forward to getting the Inner Circular.

- **Elizabeth Divver**, Group HR Director, The Big Issue Group

Sign now! The monthly Q & A sessions are invaluable, the magazine is packed full of helpful info, you get lots of goodies and the Facebook page is really informative and a useful sounding board.

- **Caroline Hitchen**, Consultant, Caroline Neal Employment Law

WWW.HRINNERCIRCLE.CO.UK

Being a member of HR Inner Circle is one of the best sources of HR information and advice, and receiving the monthly audio seminars and magazines is extremely helpful and interesting. I can't recommend becoming a member highly enough.
There is a private Facebook group which is great for asking other members advice and sharing knowledge and experiences. I have also recently attended one of the meetups that is organised by Daniel Barnett, and it was good to meet other members (and of course Daniel) in a more social setting. It was also a good opportunity to ask any questions you wanted and being able to get advice or support as to how they would deal with whatever you ask.

- **Tracey Seymour**, HR Manager (Head of Dept), Kumon Europe & Africa Ltd

The help and advice from other HR professionals on Facebook is really valuable, and quick. All the team enjoy the audio seminars and magazines for updates on current issues.

- **Catherine Larke**, Director | myHRdept.co.uk

WWW.HRINNERCIRCLE.CO.UK

For me it's a no brainer. We have a lot of really good contributors in the HR Inner Circle and it's more than a discussion forum and invaluable source of information. When combined with the magazine, the audio seminars and events, it is a complete service especially with Daniel's legal expertise always on hand.

- **Elizabeth Ince**, Self employed HR Consultant

Just join! It is invaluable with the resources you have at hand by joining the HR Inner Circle. Especially the Facebook Group where you can get advice or a different point of view that you may not have previously considered, outside of normal working hours which is very useful. Live Q&A's too.

- **Diana Wilks**, HR Manager, Go South Coast Ltd

HR can be complex because each and every issue will have its own set of individual circumstances. Being in the HR Inner Circle enables you to bounce ideas around and make sure you are considering every angle and aspect, knowing your HR Inner Circle partners will have had a similar experience to share.

- **Pam Rogerson**, HR Director, ELAS Group

WWW.HRINNERCIRCLE.CO.UK